Sages for the Ages: Book I
Donkeys on the Roof and Other Stories

MAGGID

Uri Orbach

Donkeys on the Roof
& Other Stories

Sages for the Ages: Book I

Translated by Sara Daniel
Illustrated by Igor Kovyar

Sages for the Ages, Book I:
Donkeys on the Roof and Other Stories

Maggid edition, 2010

Maggid Books
An imprint of Koren Publishers Jerusalem Ltd.

POB 8531, New Milford, CT 06676-8531, USA
POB 2455, London W1A 5WY, England
& POB 4044, Jerusalem 91040, Israel
www.korenpub.com

Published in cooperation with Beit Midrash Elul

Originally published as *Ḥakhameinu LeYameinu* (Hebrew)

Translated by Sara Daniel © Copyright 2010, Koren Publishers Jerusalem Ltd.
Illustrated by Igor Kovyar © Copyright 2010, Koren Publishers Jerusalem Ltd.

ISBN 978 1 59264 323 3, *hardcover*

A CIP catalogue record for this title is
available from the British Library

Contents

Introduction for Parents

The Aggada, perhaps best translated as Jewish folklore, is a marvelous creation of the Jewish people that has raised up and been passed down countless generations. Aggada has been generated for hundreds of years, by hundreds of authors, dating back to the era of the Second Temple in Israel, and later in Babylon. Aggada was originally passed down orally, as proverbs, parables, explanations of holy texts, and stories told on different occasions: as part of sermons in synagogues, during Torah learning in the *Beit Midrash*, during family events such as weddings, circumcisions, funerals and so on.

Over the years and centuries, stories were written down, modified and adapted, and today they are known to hundreds and thousands, scattered over the Mishna, Tosefta, Talmud Yerushalmi and Talmud Bavli, and Midrashic exegeses. Aggada was not originally collected in a separate volume, rather, its stories were interspersed among the textual interpretations, the debates of Jewish law, and the philosophy found in such literature.

Aggada has countless facets: among them are parables and proverbs, moral advice, poetry and liturgy, riddles and tall tales, textual explorations and rabbinic wisdom, and, of course, stories. Out of a myriad of stories, the tales of great men and their great deeds stand out in their beauty, truth and relevance – the tales of our sages. From these stories, where the protagonists are the great men of the age in which they lived, we learn lessons from the Torah, lessons for life, lessons about nature and, most of all, lessons about the nature of people and their culture, and how they deal with life's struggles and joys, successes and failures, laughter and tears.

The stories of Aggada accompany us throughout our lives, from birth to bereavement, and barely any human experience is left unexplored by some story – whether the experience touches on education, law, religion, food, dress, cleanliness, health, war and peace, love and hatred, truth and falsehood, charity and kindness, stealing and returning lost property, relating to what is different from us, our interaction with animals or the environment – there is always a story. And the natural is supplemented by the supernatural; to these everyday experiences, Aggada infuses stories about dreams, magic and mystery, the epic, stories of fantasy and the imagination. Aggada is a buried treasure unearthed, a gold mine, hidden from the eye but buried in plain sight.

How best can we share this fabulous wealth with our children? Maggid Books, together with Beit Midrash Elul, raised the idea of creating a new series of books for children from the ages of five to a hundred and five, from all different parts of society. Stories of Aggada were carefully selected from ancient sources and poured into sparkling new vessels, refreshed for modern readers while preserving the original spirit, adapted in the creative spirit of Aggada into a version both contemporary and timeless. Its light language and colorful illustrations are designed to draw young readers into the world of Aggada, with the belief that its beautiful lessons deserve to be presented in an equally beautiful receptacle.

Each volume in the series is dedicated to a certain subject. The stories of the first book center around the home and family – discussing homesickness and running away from home, families that stay together and families who are parted, honoring one's parents and respecting one's children, grandparents and grandchildren, neighbors, and more. Some of the tales are well-known and will be familiar to the reader, some are less well-known and some have even been rewritten for the first time.

"Aggada has a laughing face," said Hayim Nahman Bialik, who initiated the creation of *Sefer HaAggada* (*The Book of Legends*) together with his friend Y. H. Ravnitzky. The first book in our series, *Sages for the Ages*, is a collection of stories retold by Uri Orbach, in his familiar, beloved style. He fuses humor and sharp wit with wisdom and compassion, adding the occasional jest that may go right over the heads of babes but will cause adult readers to laugh out loud.

The subjects explored in the stories may well serve as a springboard for discussions between adults and children, raising issues such as the place of the home in a child's life, fulfilling goals and keeping promises, having patience and mutual respect, the dynamics of relationships, social gaps, and more. The names in each story may lead to discussions about the other stories that involve that character, or the period of history in which they lived, such as the time of the second Temple in its full glory, the time after its destruction, or during the efforts to establish alternative spiritual centers for the Jews. The original textual source is mentioned at the end of each story, enabling the reader to explore it in its original form. You are invited to embark on a journey through new and familiar territory, and to bask in the ancient, timeless wisdom of the Agadda.

Shmuel Faust
Researcher of *Ḥazal* literature and
research adviser for the *Sages for the Ages* series

There's No Place Like Home

The teacher Rabbi Yose was known for his patience. He would never leave his classroom until every last student understood the lesson. Anyone with a child who was having trouble with his studies would send him to Rabbi Yose. Boys came from all over the country to learn with him. From *all* over.

Out of all the students in his class, out of all the struggling, daydreaming, challenging students, was a boy who baffled Rabbi Yose more than any boy he had ever attempted to teach. Not a single fact seemed to penetrate his mind. He was a daydreamer who couldn't concentrate for two seconds straight, and didn't seem to understand a thing. All his teachers had already thrown their hands up in despair. He had spent more hours staring out the window than he had spent listening to his teachers. His school deemed him the most thick-minded student they had ever encountered. His head was like a fact-repelling magnet.

But Rabbi Yose had endless patience and love for all of his students. He saw that this student was having trouble in class. Rabbi

Yose could not understand how he could pour his heart into teaching him and yet nothing, but nothing would stick.

He explained a passage in the Torah once and the student didn't get it.

Twice, thrice, he explained. Nothing.

Four, five, six times. Nada.

But Rabbi Yose had patience. He didn't shout. Instead, he asked gently, "Why don't you understand? Why aren't you listening? Why aren't you concentrating?"

For the first time, the student looked at Rabbi Yose directly in the eye, and answered, "I'm homesick."

Rabbi Yose looked at the student, and asked, "Where are you from?"

"From Great Snoring," the boy replied.

Great Snoring, Great Snoring…it took Rabbi Yose several minutes to recall where that was. Then he realized that it had taken him so long to remember because it was the biggest dump-of-a-town in the country, nowhere in the middle of nowhere, a no-man's-land in Nowheresville. Great Snoring is so hot that even the camels won't stray from the air-conditioning. Great Snoring is so dusty that it's marked on the map by a little mound of sand. In Great Snoring, people talk with their mouths closed so they won't swallow any flies. In Great Snoring, the flies fly with open mouths so they can swallow the people. Okay, maybe we're exaggerating, just a bit.

Rabbi Yose had to stop himself before he said in a disgusted tone, "You live *there*?" After all, people in Great Snoring were sick of hearing jokes and rude comments about their hometown. He said carefully, "Well, what's special about where you live?"

With shining, eager eyes, the student gushed, "Great Snoring is the most wonderful place in the world! You can cook eggs on the sidewalk! (If you clean it first from all the dust.) You never need central heating! And when a baby is born, they smear his head with mashed red figs!"

"Why do they do that?" asked Rabbi Yose, trying not to laugh.

"So the mosquitoes won't eat him alive!" answered the student. "There are lots of mosquitoes because of the neighborhood swamp, but red figs keep them away. Works like a charm."

"Ah-*ha*," said Rabbi Yose, puzzled, "and you…miss it?"

"Well, I do," answered the student sadly, "because mosquitoes buzzing around me aren't nearly as bad as people buzzing around me, making fun of me. I miss the warm, clay house where my family lives; the stone home that I'm staying in is so unfriendly and cold. I love the heat, the sun, and the dust more than the wealth and the greenery around here. That's my home, where I grew up, where I played with my friends, where people understand me. Back home, Great Snoring is a place to live, not a place to make fun of."

That was the first time that Rabbi Yose had heard the student say more than two words in a row. He now understood that the student was just homesick, lonely and misunderstood. It's hard to concentrate when you're so homesick. Even if the place you're homesick for is a place with a funny name like Great Snoring. Though, come to think of it, plenty of names are funny. Imagine if you lived in Sticky End, Upper Creek, or Inner Pickle. And have you ever been to Noah Vale?

He stroked his pupil's head gently and murmured to himself, "Blessed is He who makes a place beloved to its inhabitants. God did a great kindness by making people love the place they grew up in. Even if there are better places than someone's hometown, everyone loves his home, his neighborhood, and his native city. And when you are far from home, it's hard to concentrate on your studies."

And from that day, Rabbi Yose knew how to deal with his student from Great Snoring, how to make him happy and eager to learn. They often talked about that strange village where new babies got their heads smeared with mashed figs. The student told Rabbi Yose more stories – funny, weird, but mostly special – about Great Snoring, the hole in the middle of nowhere. Telling the stories helped the student get over his homesickness, and at last he made leaps and bounds in his Torah studies. And every time the student would begin to stare out the window, Rabbi Yose would fondly pinch his cheek and ask, "So, how are the mosquitoes doing back in Great Snoring?'

Based on Midrash, Bereshit Raba 34

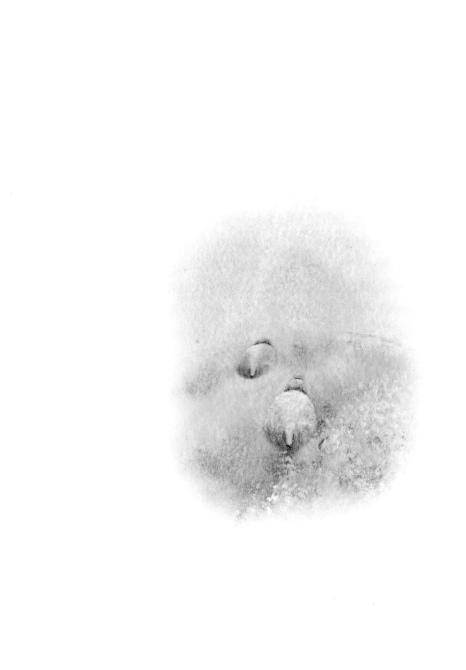

Promises Must be Kept

Akiva was a simple shepherd who worked for a very rich and generous man named Kalba Savua, which means "stuffed dog." Why was he called Mr. Stuffed Dog, you might ask? Any poor person who came to his door – even those as hungry as dogs – came out satisfied and happy. Nowadays, it's not very nice to call someone a dog, but believe it or not, the name Stuffed Dog was a compliment.

Mr. Dog had a daughter, and her name was Rachel. She was clever and beautiful and didn't have a silly nickname. As she grew, so did the list of men who wanted to marry her. Not surprising since she was bright, beautiful, and – let's not deny it – her father was one of the wealthiest men in town. In short: the perfect bride.

But out of the long list of suitors, many of them brilliant, successful, and important, Rachel fell in love with a poor, ignorant shepherd. He didn't know any Torah. He didn't have a penny to his name. He was already forty years old. But she didn't fall in love with Akiva because of his looks (outward appearances were not important to Rachel). She didn't fall in love with him because of his money (as we said, he didn't have any). She fell in love with

him because of the gentle way he handled his sheep. (Crazy as it might sound, that's why God picked Moses to take the children of Israel out of Egypt – because he was such a sensitive shepherd.) Akiva was a gentle, modest person. He had wonderful qualities. However, with all the butterflies and fireworks that he made her feel, she would only marry him on one condition:

"If I marry you," Rachel asked Akiva, "will you sell the flock and go study Torah? I think that it's a waste for you to spend your life minding sheep, while you have the potential to become a great scholar."

Akiva didn't hesitate. "Yes!"

But there was one problem. Rachel's father was a good, generous man, but he did not want his beautiful, brilliant daughter to marry one of his shepherds, especially without even asking his permission! In those days, parents would choose whom their children would marry – and more importantly, whom they would NOT marry, and whom there was *no way on God's green Earth* that they would marry. And there was *no way on God's green Earth* that Rachel would marry a simple shepherd who didn't even know how to read or write! Let the shepherd marry some Little Bo Peep. He would not marry Stuffed Dog's daughter! It may be that any poor person who came to his door would leave with a full stomach, but not everyone who came to his door could leave with his daughter!

And Rachel knew that if she dared marry Akiva, her father would disinherit her, disown her, and have nothing more to do with her.

Rachel dared, and she married Akiva.

Within a day or two, Mr. Stuffed Dog found out about their marriage. He almost fainted with anger. "She dared to marry Akiva? That ignorant shepherd! She's not my daughter anymore! I never want to see her again! Let that Akiva support her with his flock of sheep! I swear that she'll never see a single penny of all my wealth! I'll give it all to charity, and nothing to that girl who married that good-for-nothing, simple shepherd who doesn't even know how to read and write! What chutzpah!"

Mr. Dog was so angry, so insulted, so annoyed, peeved, irritable and upset that he didn't speak to a living soul for a whole week. He felt as though he had lost a daughter.

Penniless, Akiva and Rachel went to live in an old abandoned hay-shed on the outskirts of the city. The shed was freezing in winter and boiling in the summer. Akiva would pick the bits of hay out of Rachel's beautiful thick hair. She was used to sleeping on feather beds decorated with silver hangings, and now she slept fitfully on mattresses of itchy hay. Akiva did everything he could to make her feel like a queen.

"When we have money," he would tell her, "I'll craft a tiny little Jerusalem from gold, and you will wear it around your lovely neck."

But for now, they barely had two pennies to rub together. They could hardly afford to buy bread, oil, or cheese triangles. All they had was a great love for each other that helped them get through the day.

And they were happy. One day, Elijah the prophet came to them, disguised as a poor man. He knocked on their flimsy door (which was made of hay) and said to Akiva, "Sorry to bother you, but my wife just had a baby, and we'd be very grateful if you could give us a little straw for the baby's bed."

Straw was the one thing that the newlyweds had plenty of, and they happily gave their visitor a huge bundle. "You see, my dear," said Akiva to Rachel after Elijah had left, "this man is even poorer and worse off than we are. They don't even have straw to sleep on. We're doing just fine."

After a while, Rachel turned to Akiva and said, "My darling husband, it's time to fulfill your promise to me. I married you because you promised to go study Torah."

Akiva didn't hesitate. He remembered his promise and would do as his wife asked. Learning Torah was so important to Rachel that she was ready to live a hard, lonely life while Akiva studied. They both knew that love didn't necessarily mean living like a fairy tale, happily ever after. It meant making sacrifices for the other, and making each other's lives meaningful. Many years later, Akiva would become Rabbi Akiva, and would say, "Love your neighbor like yourself," which means to do everything that you would do for yourself, only for another person. They didn't yet know that he would become a great rabbi, who would say such great things, but Akiva already loved Rachel like he loved himself, and even more.

Rabbi Akiva packed up a little straw for the way – after all, it was all they had – said goodbye to Rachel and their new baby son who had been born in the meantime (mazal tov!), and set off for the faraway study house of Rabbi Eliezer and Rabbi Yehoshua. It was the first time in his life that he had sat and studied. He started by learning to read and write. Until now, he hardly knew the difference between "tomatoes" and "potatoes." Then he began to study the Torah and its interpretations. At first he learned the simpler stuff, then he began to study deeper and deeper meanings, and strung them all together like pearls on a string, until he began teaching others himself. Slowly but surely, those pearls of wisdom penetrated his mind, like tiny drops of water can wear away a solid rock, and Akiva became the great Rabbi Akiva. From a simple shepherd, his head filled with nothing but sheep and goats, he became a great teacher, full of Torah and wisdom. Now students flocked around him, instead of sheep.

But although he had learned fast, it had not happened over-night. Twelve years ago, he had arrived as a simple lonely shepherd. Twelve long years had passed since he had left his lovely Rachel and their baby boy. He had not seen them since. Rachel was still very poor and still lived in the old hay-shed. Whenever he could, Rabbi Akiva sent her the little money he had scraped together. She knew that he was growing greater and greater in Torah. Her love for him was so great that she didn't care that she lived in pov-erty – she was happy that he was fulfilling his promise to her, and many people were benefiting from his wisdom.

It was now time for Rabbi Akiva to return home. Followed by his huge flock of students, Rabbi Akiva reached his home after a long, tiring journey, and stood on the doorstep to prepare himself for meeting Rachel at last. As he stood there, he heard the voice of a neighbor talking to Rachel:

"*Ruchela*, for how long will you wait for your husband already? He has abandoned you and left you like a widow. I don't want to stick my nose into your business, but hasn't it been a bit too long? Twelve years? Who knows if he'll ever come back?"

Rabbi Akiva was about to march in and prove the "concerned" neighbor wrong, when he heard Rachel's reply:

"Oh, don't you pity me. You don't even mean it. If my husband could hear me now, I would send him back for another twelve years. Long ago, Jacob worked for our ancestor Rachel for seven years, and they felt like mere days for him, because he loved her so much. He even worked another seven years for her after that! When I think of the Torah my husband is learning, I feel as rich as a queen, and the years just fly by."

Rabbi Akiva heard these words and felt the love and faith that Rachel had in him. Rabbi Akiva didn't hesitate. He didn't even open the door to his home. To his students' surprise, he swung around

and marched all the way back to the faraway study house, without missing a beat and without stopping to rest. He didn't need rest. He had Rachel's strong love. For another twelve years he studied the Torah. He learned so deeply and intensely that he reached heights in Torah knowledge that had never been achieved before. After twelve years, which indeed flew by, he came home again, this time accompanied by thousands of students.

The whole town, proud of their famous scholar, came out to greet him as he reached the town. The neighbors said to Rachel, "Your husband is finally coming home. Don't you think you should put on a nice new dress and go out to meet him?"

Rachel was so poor that she didn't even have a new dress in honor of the occasion. But she said to her neighbors, "I don't think that after all these years, such a great man will be concerned with what I'm wearing." And she ran out to greet him.

Everyone crowded around Rabbi Akiva in excitement. Such a scholar! From their very own town! Rachel came close to him, fell down at his feet and kissed them.

All his students jumped in front of her:

"Hey, lady!"

"What's that about?"

"A little modesty, if you please!"

"No pushing, there's a line!"

They tried to shoo her off, but Rabbi Akiva, recognizing his very own Rachel, shouted, "Leave her! All my Torah that you share is hers! Everything that I learned, everything I teach, is all thanks to her. Because she gave up everything so that I could learn Torah."

And together, they went home.

So what happened to Mr. Stuffed Dog? He really did disown Rachel, his daughter, and hadn't heard from her all these years. But now, as he was growing old, he began to regret his harsh actions. He knew that Rachel was living in terrible poverty, but he had no idea that Akiva the shepherd had become the great Rabbi Akiva. He just wanted to annul his vow to never speak to her again, so that they could reunite and he could help her, after all these years.

He heard that a great rabbi was coming to town, and hoped that this celebrity could help him annul his vow.

Mr. Stuffed Dog joined the long line of people waiting to meet the great man. When it was his turn, he began to speak to Rabbi Akiva, without recognizing the man who had married his daughter over twenty-four years before. He told him how he had been angry at his daughter for marrying a shepherd who couldn't read or write. Rabbi Akiva asked him, "Tell me, sir, if you had known that the shepherd who married your daughter would learn Torah after they were married, would you still have vowed to disown her?"

"Heaven forbid!" replied Mr. Stuffed Dog. "I loved – and still love – my daughter. If I had known that her husband would try and learn Torah – or even read the weekly *parasha* sheet they have in shul! – then I wouldn't have disowned her. It just upset me that I thought she was marrying a man who would never learn a thing in his life."

"In that case," said Rabbi Akiva, "I have good news for you! I am that shepherd who married your daughter. Your Rachel only married me on the condition that I would learn Torah. She made me everything I am today."

Mr. Stuffed Dog gave a shout of joy, hugged and kissed Rabbi Akiva, and immediately moved them into a huge mansion next to his own, and gave them half of his wealth.

The very next day, Rabbi Akiva went to the best goldsmith in the town and ordered a tiny replica of Jerusalem in gold for Rachel. He came home and placed "Jerusalem of Gold" around her lovely neck. After all, a promise made must always be kept.

Based on Talmud Bavli, Nedarim 50;
Ketubot 62–63; Avot deRabbi Natan, ch. 6

Shhh! My Father is Sleeping!

A long time ago, a man lived in Ashkelon, and his name was Dama ben Netina. Dama and his family ran a double business, selling precious jewels and sparkling diamonds, and also raising herds of cattle and flocks of sheep – and they made a good living, thank you very much.

In those days – as we said before, a long time ago – the Holy Temple (*Beit HaMikdash*) was still standing in Jerusalem. The High Priest of the Temple wore a golden breastplate over his robe that was adorned with twelve jewels, one jewel for each tribe of Israel. These were not just any old jewels, but sparkling, fabulous, rare jewels, each with its own special name, just like every tribe of Israel is special.

One day, to everyone's shock and horror, the High Priest found that one of the jewels of the breastplate was missing – the jasper stone, the jewel of the tribe of Benjamin. The priests and sages searched for it everywhere, but it was not to be found. They asked people who had a jasper stone if they would donate it to the *Beit HaMikdash*, but they found no one with such a rare jewel. They offered a high sum of gold in exchange, but not a jeweler in the city had one to sell.

After a few days of searching, the priests heard that Dama the son of Netina, in faraway Ashkelon, had a precious jasper stone for sale. Dama ben Netina wasn't a Jew, and certainly didn't know that a jewel was missing from the High Priest's breastplate. He probably didn't even know that there was a breastplate at all! But business is business, and the sages immediately set off for the long journey. They collected a gleaming pile of gold to offer Dama ben Netina, wrapped it up safely and loaded the heavy sack onto their donkey for the journey. A jewel was missing from the High Priest's breastplate – there was no time to waste, and no expense must be spared!

After a long journey, the sages and their poor, tired donkey arrived at Dama's home and knocked on the door.

"Hello, Mr. Ben Netina, may we please come in? We're here on an urgent mission."

Dama invited his surprise guests in, saying, "Please sit down in the living room, only I beg you, keep your voices down. My father is taking a nap in the next room. How can I help you, my Jewish friends?"

The most senior sage cleared his throat and began, "Sir, we have come on a special mission. I'll come straight to the point: In our Holy Temple, our High Priest wears a special breastplate covered with twelve precious stones. Its jasper stone is missing and we are having trouble finding such a rare stone to replace it. We hear you have such a stone. I'll be frank, though it goes against my good business instincts – we're desperate and we're willing to pay any price for this stone. And fast – we must hurry to make it home before the Sabbath."

His friend the treasurer added, "This is a once-in-a-lifetime offer for you, sir. But there's no time to deliberate or haggle. We just give you a huge heap of gold, take the jewel, and get out of here, nice doing business with you."

Before Dama could even open his mouth, the treasurer pulled out a bulging purse, tossed it on the table, and said, "Count it! Six hundred thousand gold coins."

Dama looked from the purse, to the sages, back to the purse, and, ruefully, shook his head, "I can't."

The sages were shocked.

"Whaddya mean, you CAN'T?"

"This might sound strange, and it's really a very tempting offer, but sorry, I can't. At least, not right now."

The sages couldn't understand.

"Will you take seven hundred thousand?"

"I can't," said Dama.

"Eight hundred thousand!"

"It's out of the question."

"A million?"

"No way, Jose."

"Look, Dama, we can't force you, but you must explain why ever not. Are you very attached to your stone? Do you think it's not enough money? I mean, we offered you at least ten times the value of the stone, but we're willing to offer more, if that's what you're hinting…or is there another reason?"

Dama didn't answer. He stood up, opened a side door, peeked inside, and came back. "I'm sorry, I just can't. The jewel is indeed right here in the safe. The sum you offered is very generous, and I have no problem selling it to you at that price…"

The sages smiled. "So what's the problem? You take the money, we'll take the stone, and everybody's happy."

"Well," said Dama ben Netina, "my father's asleep."

Now the sages were really surprised by this strange man. First he tells them to keep their voices down, then he says that he can't sell them the jewel, then he says that he'd love to sell it to them but not right now, and then explains that his father is asleep – what does that have to do with anything?

Dama noticed their confusion.

"Let me explain. The key to the jewel safe is in a special purse. That purse is kept hidden under a pillow, and that pillow, for now, is propping up my father's head, and my father is fast asleep. If I take out the key, my father will wake up, and he'll be very mad. He doesn't like being woken up in the middle of his nap – to him, his nap is the most important part of the day. He even said to me once, 'Dama, dear, my nap is more precious to me than all the money in the world. I need my siesta. I don't want to be woken for any price. If I'm woken up, I become grouchy, cranky and generally unpleasant. We're a family that loves to do business, but I can't and won't do business unless I've had my nap!'"

"Well, when is he supposed to wake up?" asked the sages.

"Ay, there's the rub! You can never tell. He might wake up any moment, but it could also be in two hours or four. He has terrible trouble falling asleep, but once he's down, he's a heavy sleeper, so you just never know. Look, I can tell you're in a hurry. It's a shame to turn you down, but we have lots of money; I only have one father, and I must respect his wishes – you can't buy a good nap with all the money in the world!"

"Yes, we are very pressed for time, so we won't be able to wait for too long," said the head sage. "But we're very impressed that you won't wake your father. We appreciate the respect you have for him."

"Oh, yes," replied Dama. "Here in Ashkelon, in our family, respecting our parents is valued above all. We honor our parents, and our children honor us. Maybe thanks to that, we do so well in business. Sometimes we may miss out on a deal, but most of the time, when we show respect, we prevent arguments and cooperate, and that's why we are successful."

With no more time to spare, the sages left Dama's house in respectful silence and began the long journey back to Jerusalem. They had a feeling that they would be back to do business with Dama. Such a sensitive businessman would be sure to remove the key to the safe as soon as his father woke up, and have the stone waiting for them, whenever they came back.

The treasurer was the first to break the silence.

"I never saw such a thing. Such respect for his father! Such honor! To tell the truth, I thought he was just trying to get us to raise the price, and at the last minute he would wake up his father in order to make the deal…"

One of the other sages added, "It was worth the trip to Ashkelon just to see a man who has never learned Torah, doesn't know the Ten Commandments and probably never heard the verse "Honor your father and mother," yet shows such honor toward his father. We can learn from this man, what an important mitzva it is to honor our parents."

The very next week, the sages found another jeweler who was willing to sell them a jasper stone, and they didn't return to Ashkelon. However, after a year or two, they had an even more challenging mission. They had to find a red heifer. Since the children of Israel sinned in the desert by building a golden calf to worship instead of God, they were given the mitzva of offering a red heifer, which is a young cow. Just as our parents often clean up after us and help us make up for our mistakes, offering the red heifer atones for the sin of the golden calf. But it is no easy task to find a red cow. Most cows, as you probably know, are not red.

A jasper stone may be rare, and hard to track down. But it's nothing compared to a red cow. The sages were willing to pay a small fortune to anyone who had a pure red cow to offer. What did God do? Out of all the cows in all the barns in Israel, a red calf was born to Dama ben Netina from Ashkelon.

It wasn't long before the sages heard of Dama's red calf, and once again, they loaded up their donkey with gold and set out on the journey to Ashkelon. Once again, they arrived at Dama's door.

You're probably not surprised to hear that this time, Dama's father wasn't having a nap on top of the calf, and Dama was expecting the sages, ready to make a deal.

"I knew you'd be back," he said. "I understand that you've already found a jasper stone, but I'd be happy to sell you the calf. The asking price is exactly the price you offered me for the jasper stone. I missed out on six hundred thousand gold coins for the sake of my father's honor, but if you'll pay me that now, the cow is yours and everyone's a winner!

The sages handed him the purse without a word, and took the

red heifer with them. They were happy to find a cow that would atone for the sin of the calf, especially from a "calf" that honored his own parents!

Dama said goodbye with a friendly handshake, saying, "Maybe it's time that I told my father that because of my respect for him, we lost six hundred thousand gold coins…and got them back! I'll just go check if he's woken up yet…"

Based on Talmud Bavli, Kiddushin 31

An Uphill Struggle

Eliezer the son of Horkanos couldn't read, and he couldn't write. Horkanos, his father, was a very rich man, who had very high expectations of his children. He owned properties, many fields and vineyards, and even had the latest model horse parked in his driveway. He knew that one day, he would leave all his property to his children, so he wanted to be sure that they knew what they were doing. And he was worried about Eliezer, who wasn't learning to read and write fast enough to suit him. "Forget about that child," he thought to himself, "he's not going to amount to much. His brothers are smarter and brighter than him, they'll be the brains of the outfit. They'll run the business; he can do the donkey work. Why should he sit in class with everything going in one ear and out the other, when he can be put to practical use? *Oy*, that kid is just a financial burden."

Rather than investing in expensive private teachers for his son, or even just helping him with his homework, Horkanos took Eliezer out of school and set him to work in the fields. For year after year, Eliezer plowed and sowed and reaped away, until he was twenty-two years old. He still didn't know how to read and he still didn't know how to write. He didn't know a single mishna or a single passage of Torah. He had never read a book or even leafed through the Sunday comics, (which, to his credit, had not been invented yet). True, he was no bright spark at school, but he wasn't even up to scratch working in the fields. Everyone said he was all thumbs and no brains.

As Eliezer toiled away, his brothers learned the ropes, and when they grew up, they joined the family business. The oldest brother oversaw the vineyards, the second became responsible for the vegetable crops, the third ran the dairy, and the fourth sat in the office and did the accounting.

Each of the brothers received a plot of land on the fertile plain that surrounded the Horkanos estate. Except for Eliezer. He was the unlucky beneficiary of a particularly dry, rocky patch of land that stretched across the side of a steep hill. Even the goats had trouble grazing there. Horkanos justified this division to himself: "Eliezer is a hopeless young man. Good land would be wasted on him. It would be better for him to plow away on his hillside, not too near his brothers. I don't want him to bother them, and distract them from their useful work. He really is the black sheep of the family. *Oy*, that kid is such a financial burden…"

Poor Eliezer tried to coax his oxen across the rocky slope. It was hopeless. He sat down on a rock and began to cry.

His father, making rounds, saw him and asked, "Eliezer, why are you crying?"

Eliezer stopped crying, but didn't say a word. Horkanos, feeling guilty and sorry for his unfortunate son, said, "Well, I'll probably end up losing money for it, but you've got to make sacrifices for the kids. You can have a plot on the plain too. Just don't cry, okay?"

Eliezer moved down to the plain and started working on his new plot. A few days later, Horkanos came to see how things were moving along. He saw Eliezer sitting near his ox and again, he was crying. Now Horkanos became frustrated. "You're not a little boy anymore! You have a nice plot of land! What more could you want? Why are you crying?"

Eliezer answered him, the tears streaming down his face, "I don't want to spend my life working in a field. I want to learn. I want to learn Torah."

Now Horkanos lost his temper, and began to mock him, "You? Learn Torah? Maybe you want to try Rocket Science while you're at it? Apply to Harvard, maybe? Perhaps win a Nobel prize? You can't even read or write! For twenty-two years you haven't opened a book, now you want to sit and learn? Forget about it!"

But Eliezer wiped his tears on his sleeve and said again, "I want to learn Torah!"

Now Horkanos became livid. "You have no idea what I'm saying, do you? You are not capable of sitting and learning Torah! Do you know how much it's costing me for your keep, with you sitting like a lump, of no use to me in the business? Better you should find a girl, settle down, and send your kids to learn Torah in school. You know that your head is as thick as a brick and you're making me sick," – Horkanos had a tendency to rhyme when he was really annoyed – "and if I hear that again you'll be sent away quick! End of subject. Case closed." He turned to go, yelling as a parting shot, "And you'd better be done plowing this field by tomorrow! Finish on the double or you'll be in trouble! I didn't give you a good piece of land to sit and bawl over it, coming up with crazy ideas about learning Torah. Your behavior is intolerable! *Oy*, you're such a financial burden!"

Eliezer crumpled to his knees and wept. After a few minutes, he got up, wiped his eyes and nose on his sleeve, and pulled the plow over his ox's neck. At that moment, the ox crumpled to *its* knees, rolled over on to its side, and died.

Eliezer took this as a sign that a future in plowing was not for him. "I'll take that as a sign from Heaven that I should leave the fields and learn Torah!" He gathered up a few belongings and ran away to Jerusalem, to the study house of Rabbi Yoḥanan ben Zakkai.

Rabbi Yoḥanan, greeting him, asked, "Eliezer, have you ever learned to say the prayers, or blessings over meals?" Eliezer shook his head. He had never learned a thing. So Rabbi Yoḥanan taught him his prayers. But after a while, he saw Eliezer sitting and crying. Again.

"Why are you crying?"

"Because I want to learn more."

Rabbi Yoḥanan started slowly, teaching him two Torah laws a day. The studying was excruciatingly hard for Eliezer, who hadn't sat and learned for over twenty years. It was like plowing up a rocky hill, but he didn't give up. He became so absorbed in his studies that he didn't want to budge from his seat. For eight days straight, he didn't eat a thing. He was so deeply engrossed in his studies that he didn't feel hunger. Once in a while he absentmindedly nibbled on a pebble from the ground. He just didn't want to waste any more time eating, when he could be learning Torah. No wonder that his breath smelled funny after fasting for over a week.

Rabbi Yoḥanan marveled at Eliezer's dedication to his Torah studies. He put a friendly hand on his shoulder and said, "Go have a bite to eat, my boy. I wish for you that one day, your mouth (which smells a bit funny right now because of your commitment to Torah learning), shall speak sweet words of Torah that will draw people from all over the world."

Eliezer wept happy tears at his teacher's sweet words. Then he ate a mint.

Years passed by, and Eliezer became Rabbi Eliezer. Rabbi Eliezer became the great Rabbi Eliezer, compared in Ethics of the Fathers to a well of water that retains every precious drop. He had overcome his difficulties. At first, he was slow to grasp, but he never forgot a thing, and he built his Torah like a great marble palace with

deep, strong foundations. People indeed flocked to him, from all over the world, to hear him breathe sweet words of Torah.

Meanwhile, Horkanos was growing old. He grudgingly began to divide up his property for his sons' inheritance. His sons were eager to inherit the rich lands of their father, and thought about how they could get as much as possible. They came to Horkanos and said, provokingly, "Father, it's been many years since we've seen Eliezer. We haven't heard from him since that day when he abandoned his dead cow in the field. He has no interest in what's happening here and he hasn't lifted a finger to help run the place. We think you should ride the horse to Jerusalem, to Rabbi Yoḥanan's study house, and inform Eliezer that you're cutting him off from the inheritance!" The brothers were eager to exclude Eliezer from their father's wealth. That way, they would each get a fat quarter of the family fortune, rather than just a fifth. The father heard their "advice," mumbled to himself, "That boy. *Oy*, what a financial drain he was!" and set off for Jerusalem.

He arrived in Jerusalem and headed to Rabbi Yoḥanan's study house. He arrived just as Rabbi Eliezer had begun to speak in front of a crowd of the most honorable, rich, important people of Jerusalem. Horkanos surveyed the audience – it was filled with people that Horkanos had always dreamed of meeting (and doing business with!).

Horkanos, unseen by his long lost son, took a seat in the back and watched. As he spoke, Rabbi Eliezer's face glowed brighter and brighter, and the audience leaned forward, anxious not to miss a single word. They were giddy with admiration at his wisdom and knowledge. Horkanos quickly realized that the great Rabbi Eliezer was actually his own Eliezer, and saw how beloved and important his son had become. When Rabbi Eliezer had finished, the great Rabbi Yoḥanan rose and cried, "Happy you should be, Rabbi Eliezer, and happy should your parents be, who brought such a wonderful son to the world!"

Horkanos couldn't take it anymore. He stood up and shouted, "I am your father!"

Everyone in the room turned to him and stared as if he had just announced that he was from a galaxy far, far, away, a long, long time ago. Horkanos continued, "I must admit that I came here to cut Eliezer off from his inheritance, because many years ago, he left the house and his work without my approval. But now that I see what a scholar he's become, what an honorable man, well, I'd be proud to have *him* inherit *all* my wealth, and have *him* carry on my legacy! My other sons don't deserve a penny of it!"

Horkanos was so proud of his son's honorable position that he didn't care about disinheriting his other sons on the spot. "Those good-for-nothings," he thought to himself. "They're nothing but a bunch of financial drains. And Eliezer brings so much honor to my name, and maybe he can even put me in touch with all the right people in Jerusalem…"

But Rabbi Eliezer rose and said, "My dear father, there is no need to upset my brothers on my account. All I ask for is an equal share to theirs. Just as the Torah is equally open to all, waiting for anyone who chooses to study it, children should be treated equally by their parents. You have plenty of wealth for all of us. Personally, I don't really need any riches, as the Torah is more precious to me than all the gold and silver in the world. All I want is for you to love me as much as you love my brothers."

Now Horkanos realized that he had treated Eliezer unfairly. He regretted that he hadn't used some of his wealth to get his son an expensive private tutor, one that would have helped him get started before the age of twenty-two. And, perhaps because he was now angry at himself, Horkanos couldn't help but rhyme:

"My kid was a pain; a financial drain. But open the champagne, 'cause now he's a brain!"

Based on Midrash, Bereshit Raba 42;
Avot deRabbi Natan, ch.6; Pirkei deRabbi Eliezer, ch.2

The Most Precious Thing
in the World

A long, long time ago in a small, pretty town on the shore of the Kinneret, there lived a man and a woman. They had plenty of money, many rich, fertile fields, vineyards that grew heavy with juicy wine grapes, servants, horses and donkeys, and a little summer house in Lebanon where they liked to get away from it all. For ten years they had lived together with great riches and great happiness. But there was one blot on their happy life. God had not blessed them with children.

Money can do a lot, almost everything. But it can't buy rain, it can't bring the dead back to life, and it can't bless a couple with children. They went to the best doctors, tried the best treatments, prayed at the graves of the greatest, most righteous people – but nothing helped. They loved each other very much, but without children, they just weren't happy. "If only I had a child, a little child to love," prayed the woman every evening, as the sun set over the sea.

The husband thought to himself, "I love my wife so much, but if after ten years, a couple has no children, they must separate. If she marries someone else, God may bless her with a baby."

The wife thought to herself, "I love my husband so much, but perhaps if we separate and he marries another woman, God may bless him with a baby."

They decided to go seek advice from Rabbi Shimon bar Yoḥai. The great wise sage lived not far off, next to Safed. The husband thought to himself, "If we must divorce, then we should do so only through Rabbi Shimon. I want to be sure that it's the right thing to do, and he's the very best and wisest sage. We always choose the best of everything, and that includes rabbis!" The wife thought to herself, "Divorce? *Oy*. If we must. But only through Rabbi Shimon. Our family always goes to him for advice. If we must divorce, then only with Rabbi Shimon's name on the certificate, so I will know that we made the right decision."

They had the servants load up their best donkey, packed some snacks for the way – some pieces of watermelon and a bag of sunflower seeds to nibble on, along with a bottle of water, sun hats, a roadmap and sunscreen – and they were off, servants in tow.

A couple of hours later, they reached Rabbi Shimon's house. He was sitting on his porch, swaying over a pile of ancient books and nibbling on a piece of carob. He welcomed them with open arms. He listened sadly as they told him their story. He understood that they didn't want to part, but they wanted to give each other a second chance at raising a family.

Rabbi Shimon said, "This is truly a delicate matter. On the one hand, you don't really want to leave each other. On the other hand, you both long to have children. You've been to a doctor?"

"Of course," replied the woman. "We've been to several doctors, all experts on the subject."

"Good," said Rabbi Shimon. "We must always try to do what we can, as well as praying and asking rabbis. I can only try and give you advice and encouragement and pray for you. But I have a question: When you married ten years ago, you made a big fancy wedding, with dancing, catering, the whole smorgasbord. Right?"

"Oh yes, and it was a beautiful wedding. My parents were so happy," said the woman, as a fat tear welled up in her right eye.

"A big wedding with all the trimmings. Everyone came – they all danced like crazy," sighed the husband, as a small tear stung his left eye.

Now Rabbi Shimon said something which left them gaping like codfish at the fishmonger's. "Very good. I suggest that you go home, together, and prepare a similar feast in honor of your divorce! With fancy shmancy catering. And music. I'd keep the guest list small, but throw the party properly. Just as you celebrated your wedding with joy, celebrate your separation with joy. With a lot of good wine – I'm stressing the good wine here – with a band, a photographer, the whole works. And part with joy and good wishes."

Rabbi Shimon's words seemed strange indeed, but the couple asked no questions. Instinctively, they followed his advice. After all, they didn't want to part, and if Rabbi Shimon advised them

to make a feast for the occasion, then maybe he knew something that they didn't.

They arrived home, happy to have something to distract them from their sorrows. They made a party, a feast like their wedding ten long years before. The guests even brought gifts. The band played their best, carefully avoiding all the usual wedding songs about grooms rejoicing over their brides and building homes together, and the photographer snapped away as the wife plied her husband with wine, wine and more wine. When the husband's heart was merry with all the wine, his cheeks red and his eyes very slightly out of focus, he waved his hand majestically in the air and said, "My dear wife, or, should I say, my dear soon-to-be-ex-wife, now that you're going back to your parents' home, where I took you from so – hic! – many years ago, you may take back from my house the nearest and dearest thing – hic! – to your heart. Whatever you want, my darling; horses, servants, whatever you fancy, shall be yours for evermore!"

She offered him yet another cup of good red wine, and he sunk into a deep sleep, his cheek resting on a piece of divorce cake.

When the guests had gone, and the husband was still fast asleep at the table, the wife turned to her servants and said, "Now, quickly but carefully, carry my husband and have him brought to my parents' home."

"After that 'divorce feast,' I'm not surprised by anything," muttered the butler to the gardener. Between them, they lifted the sleeping man onto his bed, and then proceeded to carry him to his father-in-law's house a couple of kilometers down the road.

When the husband awoke in the middle of the night, after the wine had worn off, he sat up in shock and said, "Dear, where am I?"

"In my parents' house," she said.

"What do you mean, 'In your parents' house?' Why should I be here? Why aren't I at home?"

"Well," she replied, "last night you told me that I could take whatever is nearest and dearest to my heart back to my parents' home. Well, I thought it over, and came to the conclusion that *you* are the nearest and dearest to my heart. So I took you."

A tiny tear welled up in her right eye, and a big tear splashed down his left cheek.

As dawn rose, together they loaded up their donkey and journeyed back to Rabbi Shimon.

Rabbi Shimon, sitting on his porch, swaying over his books, chewing his carob, watched as their silhouette grew bigger against the pinkish sky. He rose to greet them, moving his lips in prayer: "Master of the universe, please fulfill this couple's dreams and fill their arms with children. Now, as the husband brings back his wife from her father's home, like a bridegroom bringing his bride to their new home, open Your heart to their renewed love and bless them with happiness and fruitfulness."

And then his lips moved with prayers more holy and secret, and the tears flowed from both of his eyes and streamed down both of his cheeks.

The man and his wife returned home, with renewed love and renewed hope. Rabbi Shimon's prayers for the couple reached the heavens, and within a year, they held a new baby in their arms.

Based on Midrash, Shir HaShirim Raba 1

Donkeys on the Roof

A long, long time ago, a little boy named Elazar grew up in a village in the north of Israel. When we say grew, we really mean it. The little boy grew and grew until he wasn't little at all. He was twice the size of the other kids in his class. He was the tallest, the strongest, the biggest, and the widest boy in the whole school. And the whole village. And the whole country.

The other kids didn't tease him, though. They had all grown up together – well, maybe he had grown a little faster than them. But as well as being big, and tall, and wide, he also had a gentle heart, and he always helped everyone out, and everyone loved him. And, not surprisingly, he was always picked first in gym class.

His father, Rabbi Shimon Bar Yoḥai, was proud of him, but his mother was more than proud of him.

"Oh, my strong little man! Here, have another bagel! And I've just baked these cookies for you! And this loaf of bread is fresh out of the oven; eat, eat, eat!"

Elazar had the most voracious appetite. His mother was always urging him to eat all his dinner so that he would grow big and strong. It was working, so far.

He loved eating, and he loved learning Torah. Boy, did learning Torah make him hungry. And Jews are commanded to learn Torah "all day and all night," so you can imagine just how hungry he was most of the time.

He would polish off pretzels as he pondered the Parasha.

He would munch on marshmallows as he memorized mishnayot.

He would scoff salty snacks as he studied the sayings of the sages.

And he would wash everything down with a nice glass of milk or four as he told his father what he'd learned in school.

In years to come, he would become the great Rabbi Elazar. He was a widely renowned Torah scholar and a widely waisted man. When the Romans wanted to kill the great Torah scholars across Israel, he hid with his father Rabbi Shimon Bar Yoḥai in a cave for thirteen years, with nothing but carobs to eat and water to drink. So it's a good thing that he had filled up on his mother's cakes all those years.

But let's go back to Rabbi Elazar when he was just Elazar, the not-so-little boy. His favorite place to learn Torah was in his mother's kitchen. She would take loaf after golden loaf out of the oven and set it down by her son as he swayed back and forth over his books. He would stop swaying in between lines and take a huge bite of warm crusty bread, wash it down with a swig of chocolate milk, and learn another verse or two. His mother was so proud of her little scholar that she couldn't always restrain herself and would run up to her son, give him a tight squeeze and say, "Oh, my little Torah scholar! Have another roll! You have to keep your strength up so you can learn more Torah! And here, have a nice chocolate milkshake!"

Back in those days, diets hadn't yet been invented.

Thanks to all those yummy bagels – though it was really thanks to all the effort he put into his studies – Elazar soon became the best student in the class.

One day, a band of traders came to town, and passed by Rabbi Shimon's house. Rabbi Shimon owned some fields next to his house, and the traders were interested in buying his crops. As they were tying their donkeys to the fence, they saw not-so-little

Elazar sitting outside on the porch, reading a book, with a huge pile of crusty rolls next to him on a tray. Mesmerized, they watched as he swallowed roll after roll. They didn't know that he was the best student in his class. They didn't know that he was a gentle, kind person. All they saw was a mountain of a kid, stuffing his mouth with bread as if there was no tomorrow.

"Whoa! Look at that kid," said one of the traders to his friends. "He has the appetite of a whole family."

"Oh yeah," said the second. "Hey, chubby, if you keep eating like that, you're going to cause a national famine!"

They burst out laughing.

"Incredible," said the third. "It's like there's a huge snake in his stomach, gobbling up everything the kid puts away. Incredible, incredible…"

Elazar didn't say a word. He had been happily reading his book and hadn't even noticed the traders until the "Hey, chubby" comment. He knew he looked different from everyone, but he still had feelings. Everyone who knew him, loved him regardless of – and even because of – his size, but nonetheless, it hurt to be made fun of, even by strangers.

He didn't say a word, but when the traders went into the house, he untied all ten donkeys, slung them over his shoulder, and one by one, carried them onto the roof. He was no weakling, that Elazar. At the tender age of five he had helped his mother by schlepping half-ton bags of flour to the kitchen (so she could make a nice snack for the little dear), so what was a donkey or two? Within a few minutes, ten confused donkeys were braying on the roof of the house, and Elazar resumed his place on the porch and happily went back to reading and munching. He had to keep his strength up, after all.

After an hour or so, the traders came out of the house.

"Where are our donkeys?" they shouted. "Who took them?"

They heard braying echoing down from the roof, and looked up.

"Whoa! How did they get up there? Hey kid, did you see who… wait…it must have been you! Why the…"

Elazar didn't say a word, and kept on munching, not bothering to look up from his book. The traders banged on Rabbi Shimon's door, and shouted,

"Rabbi Shimon, your kid put our donkeys on the roof! How can we bring them down? How can we load them up with merchandise?"

Rabbi Shimon eyed them suspiciously.

"He is a very good boy, you know. Did you say anything to him? Did you upset him in some way?"

The traders started looking down and shuffling their feet.

"Well, I don't know if you'd call it *upsetting*…"

"We just watched him eat…like…a whole bakery."

"But did you say anything?" Rabbi Shimon persisted.

"Well, sort of. We were only kidding. I said it looked like there was a hungry snake in his stomach that made him gobble up so much food."

"I did call him chubby," the other conceded. "And I said that if he kept eating, he would cause a famine…" he added, his voice trailing off.

"Well, that sounds insulting to me," Rabbi Shimon said. "Friends, why do you care if the kid sits and enjoys himself? He's not eating *your* crops. *You're* not expected to feed him. Who's providing for him, you or me?"

"Listen, Rabbi Shimon," said one of the traders. "We didn't know he was so sensitive. We didn't mean for him to be so insulted. And we certainly didn't think that he was able to carry the donkeys all the way to the roof."

Rabbi Shimon furrowed his brow and said, "God created food for the world, and gives it out as He sees fit. It's not your problem to worry about how much Elazar eats. And excuse me, but I don't think that it's very polite to make such remarks to a child who isn't yours and isn't harming you in any way. Why do you have to comment on how much he's eating? But because you seem like decent fellows who certainly regret their momentary lapses of courtesy, you can go out to the porch and tell little Elazar that his father requests that he bring the donkeys back down."

The traders went out to the porch, apologized to Elazar, and said, "Your father requests that you please, please, please bring the donkeys back down."

When he heard the word "father," Elazar looked up from his book, put down his half eaten roll, and ran to the roof. He loved and respected his parents, just like they loved and took care of him, and he always fulfilled the mitzva of honoring his father and mother.

This time, he slung a donkey over each shoulder, and in five short trips, ten confused donkeys were munching rolls on the porch. He was so eager to obey his father that he barely felt their weight. The traders watched with gaping mouths, but were careful not to say a thing.

They loaded up their donkeys and slunk out of the house, having learned a thing or two about watching their tongues.

Elazar sat back down on the porch, and his proud mother brought him another tray of pastries, warm and fresh from the oven, so that he'd have the strength to learn Torah.

Based on Pesikta deRav Kahana 11

There's Always Time for Grandchildren

Rabbi Yehoshua loved to learn and teach Torah with all of his students. He loved it so much – and was loved so much – that wherever he went, he was surrounded by students. *Wherever* he went – not only was he surrounded in the classroom and the *Beit HaMidrash*, but his students followed him to places where people don't usually learn Torah – to the marketplace, the town square, the pool and the train station (there was a train station back then, with a huge sign saying "Under Construction," and the train was added two thousand years later). They even followed him home, so his wife made sure to always leave a jug of milk and a plate of cookies on the doorstep so he wouldn't have to let them all into the house.

Rabbi Yehoshua was a very busy man. Imagine having *several hundred* students who all want to ask you *just one question* or tell you *just one story* and speak to you for *just one minute*. That adds up to hundreds of minutes, and there are only one thousand, four hundred and forty minutes in a day! Most of these minutes were taken up by eating, sleeping and teaching so, not surprisingly, Rabbi Yehoshua did not have much time for anything else.

But no matter how busy he was, or how many students were chasing him down the street to ask him about a mishna, there was one thing he never, ever missed. Every Friday, between 2:22 p.m. and 3:22 p.m., Rabbi Yehoshua sat in his study at home with his grandson, Shuki.

Shuki was a very good student. Every day he learned with his friends at school, and sometimes even after school. But his very favorite thing was his special hour of learning with his grandfather. He would run from school to his grandparents' house, help his grandmother sweep the kitchen, taste from all the bubbling pots on the stove, and greet his grandfather at the door as he came home from the *Beit Midrash*. All the yeshiva students who had followed Rabbi Yehoshua home would watch Shuki enviously as Rabbi Yehoshua said "Shabbat Shalom" and closed the door, wishing *they* were his grandchild.

Shuki felt very proud and privileged. At exactly 2:22 p.m., the two of them sat in Rabbi Yehoshua's study, with the sets of holy books with their gleaming gold letters, towering on the shelves around them, and delicious smells sneaking under the door from the kitchen. His grandfather would ask Shuki what he had learned that week, and Shuki would tell him. Shuki would ask his grandfather what he had taught that week, and Grandpa Yehoshua would explain. Then they would learn a mishna together – working their way through the six books of Mishna – and as they finished, Grandma would come in and give him a freshly baked, peanut-butter cookie, still warm from the oven, place another in his school bag for later, and say, "Shuki dear, go home and send love and kisses to Mom, Dad and the little ones, and Shabbat Shalom!"

And Shuki, with a warm and fuzzy feeling, and a warm and crumbly cookie, would set off for home, already looking forward to next week. His grandfather, from his study window, would watch him trot down the path, until the inevitable knock on his door at 3:24 from one of the students who had been lining up since 3:00.

Rabbi Yehoshua also looked forward to every Friday afternoon with Shuki. He would not give up this special time for all the world. He never missed a week, never postponed, never forgot, never even showed up a minute late –

Until one week…It had been a ridiculously hectic morning since he had risen at dawn. The market was packed and his old donkey had stalled, and he had to schlep the shopping himself after taking the donkey to the garage, and he was ten minutes late for his morning class, and he spent half an hour dealing with a halakhic emergency, and he tried to prepare for his Shabbat lecture but important visitors had dropped in from out of town, and he had to deal with a dispute between two farmers and then he dropped an envelope with money for Shabbat food in his poor neighbor's mailbox, and ran to the bathhouse, panting.

These were the days before anyone, rich or poor, had the plumbing for a bath in the comfort of their own home. Instead, on a Friday, everyone would go to the bathhouse or to a local spring in order to prepare for Shabbat.

That afternoon, Rabbi Yehoshua arrived, breathless, at the bathhouse and began hurriedly to remove his shoes and clothes and stack them neatly in a pile. Just as he was about to step into the water and begin lathering up, he happened to glance at the nearest sundial. Fourteen minutes past two! In eight minutes he was supposed to be sitting in his study with Shuki! And here he was, undressed in the bathhouse! How could he have forgotten their weekly learning session? How could he disappoint his favorite grandson? With barely a moment's hesitation, Rabbi Yehoshua jumped back into his clothes, whisking on his tzitzit and briskly buttoning his shirt. He sprang into his shoes and catapulted his kippa onto his head.

His good friend, Rabbi Ḥiya, shot him a confused glance and said, "Hey, Rabbi Yehoshua. Isn't it customary to wash *before* you leave the bathhouse?"

"Don't ask," replied Rabbi Yehoshua, buckling his belt. "I learn with my grandson every Friday, 2:22 on the dot. And this week, I completely forgot…"

Rabbi Ḥiya, choosing this moment to start an interesting debate, said, "But Rabbi Yehoshua, didn't you yourself once teach that once you've started something, you can finish it – for example, if a man begins to prepare for the bathhouse, and suddenly remembers that he hasn't prayed yet, then he may first finish washing, and then go to pray?"

"That's true, and I'm glad that you remember what I teach," replied Rabbi Yehoshua, tying his shoelaces, "but learning Torah with my grandson is even more important than having a shower."

"More important?" Rabbi Ḥiya began to ponder, not noticing Rabbi Yehoshua was in a hurry. "But surely you can be a little late. Your grandson isn't yet a busy person like you are. Isn't it more efficient to have a quick wash, now that you're here, and learn with him half an hour later?"

"He may be a little boy," answered Rabbi Yehoshua, who had mastered the art of sounding like he had all the time in the world while simultaneously gathering up his things and getting ready to zoom off, "but how can I teach him the importance of not wasting a minute if I show up late, if I don't value *his* time? Besides, learning with your grandson is like standing at Mount Sinai and receiving the Torah directly from God's mouth."

"That sounds interesting!" said Rabbi Ḥiya. "How so?"

"You remember the verse 'And you shall tell your sons and sons of sons, of the day you stood before God at Ḥorev'? This verse mentions grandparents learning with their grandchildren, together with the day we received the Torah at Mount Ḥorev, which is Mount Sinai. From this we understand that learning with your children and grandchildren is like receiving the Torah from God, otherwise the two wouldn't be mentioned together. And you want me to finish my shower and be late for *Matan Torah*?"

"Wow, that's..." began Rabbi Ḥiya, but Rabbi Yehoshua was long gone, halfway down the street before Rabbi Ḥiya had closed his mouth.

Rabbi Yehoshua arrived at his front door at 2:21, panting furiously. As he was opening the front door, Shuki ran up the driveway, also panting furiously. The two of them stood in the doorway, catching their breath and grinning at each other.

"Grandpa," said Shuki, when he could finally speak, "there was a big basketball game after school today, between my team and another school. The games are usually on Thursday, but it was moved to today this week. With all the excitement I almost forgot to come…and I remembered just before the final quarter – our team was one point ahead, it was really close – but I didn't care, I ran all the way here!"

Rabbi Yehoshua was very relieved that he had given up his shower. Imagine if he had been late, when Shuki had missed the end of the game and run all the way to his house…how would they both have felt, then?

"I'm so glad that our time is so important to you, Shuki," he said, as they walked into the study. "Would you believe it, this week I almost forgot, too?"

Shuki laughed, then looked at his grandfather more closely.

"Grandpa, why do you have soap in your hair?"

Based on Talmud Yerushalmi, Shabbat 1:2

A Father's Surprise

Many years ago, there lived a wise man who was known to all as Rabbi Ḥama Bar Bissa. Rabbi Ḥama wanted to study Torah in the best place possible, from the most learned sages possible, together with the best students possible. Rabbi Ḥama had a family that he loved; a wonderful wife and a tiny, new baby boy. He kissed them both on the cheek and said, "My dear wife and my dear son, my whole life I have wanted to learn Torah. I am going to travel to the faraway city and steep myself in Torah, so that I may hope to return to you as a wise, learned man."

His wife didn't object, or even ask any questions. She didn't say, "But our baby was only just born, won't you stay a little longer?" In those days it was common for people to travel far away in order to earn money or learn Torah in the best place for them. Nowadays people still travel all over the world to earn money and learn Torah, and they can keep in touch with their families. But back then there were no buses or cars, no phones or computers, and people sometimes came home only once or twice a year, without having spoken to their families all the while. The Torah was the most important part of their lives, and they were willing to make sacrifices to study it.

So Ḥama bar Bissa set off for a kingdom far, far away to study Torah. The kingdom was so far, far away that he never took a vacation to visit his family. For twelve long years, without a single vacation, he sat from sunrise until the moon set, and swayed over holy books. He barely ate and drank and instead, hungrily consumed the words of the Torah and thirstily drank in its knowledge.

After twelve intense years, he slowly and thoughtfully closed his books. "My boy Oshaya is soon to be a Bar Mitzva. It's time to go home. I've been away for almost his whole life, but like any father, I must prepare my boy for his Bar Mitzva. I have to teach him to read from the Torah, prepare a *devar Torah* with him that he'll say in shul, and share my learning with him so that he will understand the importance of the Torah. I haven't been around, so he probably doesn't know enough Torah." He packed up his books, gathered up his few possessions, and set off for the long way home.

After weeks of weary walking, as the sun sank down low into the sea, he approached the edge of his town. He didn't want to shock his wife by showing up unannounced on the doorstep. There were a few well-known cases of people returning and wanting to surprise their families, but surprising them a little too well, so that they fainted dead away. He had been too busy learning Torah to have time to learn first aid as well.

So Rabbi Ḥama went into the local *Beit Midrash*. There he was sure to meet a neighbor who would tell his wife that her newly-returned husband would be home after the evening prayer. He sat down, pulled out his books, and resumed his learning.

After a while, a young boy walked into the *Beit Midrash*. It happened to be Oshaya, Rabbi Ḥama's very own son, but the father obviously didn't recognize his son, and the son certainly didn't

recognize his father! Rabbi Ḥama rose out of respect for the boy.
That was the local custom – those who sat learning stood to greet
others who came to learn, no matter their age. Rabbi Ḥama, interested to talk to a boy around the age of his son, started asking all
the usual questions that grownups like to ask:

"What grade are you in?"

"What are you learning in class?"

"What does Rashi say about that?"

"What does Rambam say about *that*?"

"What do our sages say about an ox who gored a cow?"

"And what does the law have to say about two who hold a prayer shawl and both claim that it's theirs?"

The boy was intelligent and answered well, and soon the questions became harder and harder. Rabbi Ḥama asked and the boy answered. He challenged and the boy rose to the challenge. He was surprised by this clever, sweet boy.

"I've never met such a little genius! He's answered all of my questions; even difficult ones, things that usually only adults know – the boy answered them all."

If he had only asked the simplest question of all – "What's your name, child?" – he would have been even more surprised…

He thought to himself, "Maybe it's a shame that I was away for all those years. If a boy can become so learned and sharp even in a small town like this, then I could have taught my own son to learn like this boy, and maybe he would have been just as learned…"

Lost in his thoughts, Rabbi Ḥama said goodbye to the boy, and began to make his way home. He knocked on the door like he used to (so his wife would know it was him), and slowly opened it. His wife welcomed him joyfully. It had been twelve long years. Minutes after this happy reunion, Oshaya came in. Rabbi Ḥama saw him and rose in respect for the little *talmid ḥakham*, like one stands when an important person enters a room. He didn't understand what this clever boy was doing in his home!

His wife watched them both and asked, "Ḥama, why did you stand up when your son came in? Shouldn't it be the other way round – Oshaya is supposed to stand for you!"

Rabbi Ḥama almost fainted on the spot. "This is Oshaya? The boy from the *Beit Midrash* who answered all of my questions…this is my Oshaya?"

He grabbed the boy in a huge bear hug and turned to his wife. "My dearest, I am so happy to be back, and so thrilled that our son received *such* an education! I left home for twelve years so that I would be able to teach our son when I came back – now I see that Oshaya should be the one to teach me!"

"Well, my dear husband," answered Mrs. Bar Bissa. "For twelve years we waited for you, and I made sure that Oshaya would keep up his learning, even without his father around. I didn't want him to miss out and be behind just because his father was away. Every evening, while you sat so far away and learned Torah, we sat right here and kept the seats in your study warm while we learned Torah. Every morning, while you sat on that yeshiva bench so far away, Oshaya sat on the school bench here and learned. I knew that you would come back with great knowledge in Torah, and I wanted our son to be great in Torah as well, so you could learn together when you came back. Tomorrow morning, God willing, you will sit together and learn together at last!"

Rabbi Ḥama was so happy, and said excitedly, "I'm ready to learn with you right now! Why wait until tomorrow?"

Based on Talmud Bavli, Ketubot 62

In the Soup

Many years ago, there lived a man called Rav. He was a learned man, well known for his wisdom, and people would come to him from near and far to ask his advice. He taught Torah, settled arguments between friends and enemies, advised married couples how to live together happily and peacefully, showed parents how to help their children with homework, and helped people help themselves.

The ironic thing was, that Rav spent so much time helping others help themselves that he forgot to help *himself*! He was so concerned about the harmony in other people's homes that he didn't see a storm brewing in his own household.

His wife would complain, "Great, just great. It's very good of you to spend so much time helping, everywhere but here. You know, it would be nice to see you once in a while. Maybe if I make an appointment…"

Rav would look down at his knees and awkwardly ask for his favorite pea soup. After a long day, he was always in need of a good meal. His wife was a fabulous cook.

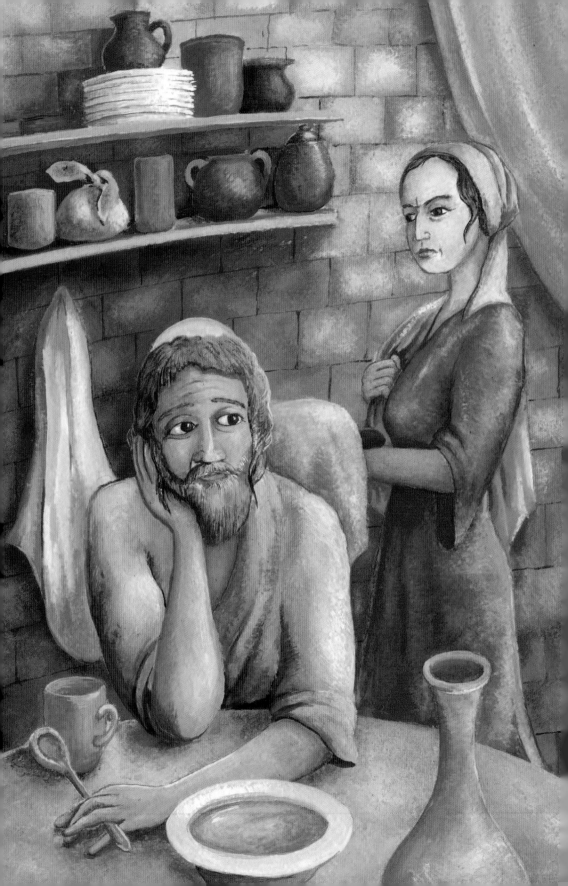

So it went on, day after day. Rav would come home late, after the children were all asleep, having spent the day helping people – and in his own home, his children barely saw their father.

Rav's wife was just sick of the whole situation. He had married *her*, not the whole town. She supported his important work, but she also wanted to see her husband once in a while! It was all very well that Rav was a famous lecturer on how to raise and teach children, but she felt that he needed to come home and actually spend time with his children, rather than spend all his waking hours talking about it to others. She was single-handedly taking care of the house and the children, and on top of it all, she had to cook pea soup every night, after putting the kids to bed and cleaning up after *their* dinner!

"If Rav pretends not to hear my requests to come home a little earlier," she said to herself, "well, I'll pretend not to hear him."

When Rav came home that night, she didn't complain about how late it was. But when he asked her for some pea soup, she went to the kitchen, and came back with a bowl of lentil soup. Rav ate his soup in silence, thinking she had made a mistake. But the soup was delicious – so the next night, Rav asked her for lentil soup. Imagine his confusion when she brought him a bowl of pea soup instead! On Tuesday, he asked for chicken. She brought him meatloaf. If the way to a man's heart is indeed through his stomach, then his wife was obviously out to do battle!

After a few days, Rav realized that his wife was purposely bringing him food he hadn't asked for. She was angry at him. The evenings became more and more tense – he would come home late and exhausted, his wife would barely say a word to him, and bring him food that he didn't ask for. He didn't know what to do. His job was so demanding, and the people needed him so much – how could he come home earlier?

Meanwhile, Ḥiya, Rav's oldest son, was growing up. He was his mother's biggest help around the house, and a bright and hard-working student. Being a sensitive boy, he could tell that something unpleasant was happening in his home, and something had to be done about it. One night, as his tired father opened the front door, Ḥiya (the only one of the children who was still up) ran up to him before his mother caught wind of his arrival, and asked him, "Hi, Abba! What would you like Imma to make you for dinner?"

"Hmmm. I'd like some pea soup, please."

Ḥiya ran to the kitchen. "Imma, Abba just came home, please make him lentil soup for dinner!" His mother sighed and began to prepare…pea soup. Ḥiya smiled. Success!

Every day, Ḥiya would wait nervously for his father to come home, ask him what he wanted for dinner, and run to tell his mother. If his father said lentil soup, he would change the order to pea soup. If his father asked for meatloaf, he would tell his mother to make chicken. If his father requested salmon, he would craftily ask for trout. It was fortunate for him that his mother was pretty predictable. After a few days, Rav said happily to his wife, "My dear, thank you so much for making what I asked for. It really makes me happy that you've forgiven me for my busy schedule."

A confused look flitted across her face, and she looked down at the couscous that she had made after Ḥiya had asked her to make rice. "But I haven't been making what you asked for!" she replied. Ḥiya, guiltily playing with his soup, said, "Abba, Imma, the truth is, it was me. I saw that you were making Abba different food, and I thought that by telling you something different, then you'd make him what he wants."

The parents looked at each other and couldn't help but smile.

"Ḥiya," said Rav, "I always knew you were a bright one. It's true

that parents can learn a lot from their kids. I should have thought of that one myself!"

But then his voice became serious, and he continued, "But Ḥiyaleh, don't do that anymore. I know you meant well, but you're really learning to lie. If I say that I would like pea soup, and you tell Imma that I want lentil soup, then you're lying. You're turning the world upside down. And even though it may set a tiny detail straight, everything else slides around. If your mother isn't cooking what I asked for, that's her way of telling me that something's wrong. And if she makes me what I do ask for, then I think that everything's okay even when it's not. And now, my clever boy, go and get me a piece of your mother's excellent apple pie. And I don't mean chocolate brownies!"

While Ḥiya was in the kitchen, Rav took his wife's hand, and said, "I'm sorry, my dear. Children should never have to mediate between their parents. I do see that I need to be around more – if we have dinner as a family, there'll be no more problems of mixed up orders…"

From that day on, Rav made sure to be home in time for dinner with the family, before the children had to go to bed. At first, he had to write *"Family Dinner: Interpersonal relationship counseling,"* in his appointment book, to remember and to justify leaving work early, but with time, he saw how happy his wife and children were, and enjoyed it so much himself, that he was rarely late. He realized that he needed to practice what he preached to others. After all, charity begins at home.

Based on Talmud Bavli, Yevamot 63

This Halla is Divine!

Rabbi Ḥanina ben Dosa was a very poor man. He didn't even have enough money for ḥallot for Shabbat. He was a great man who spent a great deal of time praying for others, but never for himself. Every Friday, the women of the neighborhood would fill up their ovens with rich dough, but Rabbi Ḥanina's wife would only gaze sadly at her empty oven. Fluffy smoke and delicious smells rose from every chimney in the neighborhood. Every chimney that is, but Rabbi Ḥanina's.

Every week, Rabbi Ḥanina's wife was flushed with shame. She could cope with hunger, but she couldn't cope with the gossip they spoke about her behind her back. (Have you ever played hide-and-seek with a two year old? They cover their face and think that *you* can't see *them*. That's how it is with gossipers. They can't see your face, and so they think that you can't hear them.)

"That Ḥanina, always praying, while his children go hungry."

"Why doesn't he find a proper job?"

"*Oy*, the poor woman. She probably just can't bake to save her life."

Stinging, spiteful words. She couldn't take it anymore.
So what did she do?

One Friday morning, she filled her oven up with twigs. They began to burn and at last, smoke was curling out of her chimney too. Anything to quiet the wagging tongues of the neighbors. As everyone knows, there's no smoke without fire, and why should someone fire up their oven if it's empty?

But one of the neighbors didn't want to leave poor Mrs. Ben Dosa alone. She noticed the smoke rising out of the Ben Dosa family's chimney and turned to her husband with a mocking smile.

"Who is that woman trying to fool? What, does she think I'm stupid or something? Anyone can see that her oven is empty. That's just plain wood smoke. There's no baking smell! What, she thinks that she can trick us into thinking that she has something to bake?"

Her husband looked up from his paper and said, "What do you care what there is or isn't in their oven? Maybe the poor wretches scraped a few coins together and bought a little flour for ḥallot? Honestly, Griselda, leave them alone."

"Oh, you men, you don't understand anything!" she replied. "I'm going to see exactly what she's cooking up there. I've been baking, cooking and frying for forty years, and no one is going to convince me that you can make bread out of twigs!"

She stormed out of the house and knocked on Mrs. Ben Dosa's door.

Mrs. Ben Dosa heard her knock and rushed up to the roof balcony. She pretended not to hear. All she needed now was some neighbor poking her nose into her oven that was filled with nothing but smoke. She was sick of the neighbors talking.

You can pick your friends, and you can pick your nose, but you can't pick your neighbors. (Or your neighbor's nose.) There are some neighbors who sneak through the door like a cold draft, and before you know it, the children have caught a cold. Griselda was that kind of neighbor. Curiosity didn't just kill the cat, it also opened the door for her. She went into the kitchen and called out in a helpful sort of way, "Oh, Mrs. Ben Dosa, your ḥallot are burning! Your rolls are getting black! Your cakes are catching fire!"

She had started saying this just to be nasty. But suddenly, there

was a miracle. As she watched, the oven filled up with huge golden ḥallot, crispy rolls, and fantastic twisty yeast cakes. A miracle! In wonder, Griselda called out again, "Quickly, quickly! Bring your peel!" (A peel is the long flat shovel that bakers use to take things out of a brick oven. Back when everyone had big brick ovens, they all had peels.)

Mrs. Ben Dosa heard the change in her neighbor's voice, and peeked downstairs. She saw the oven swelling with golden dough, composed herself for a moment, and came downstairs with the peel in her hand.

"Oh, it's nice of you to come, Griselda, I was just upstairs fetching my peel; the ḥallot are ready. I think I made more than usual this week. Maybe you'll take a few? My ḥalla recipe is just divine!"

She held out the fresh warm ḥallot and Griselda, in complete shock, thanked her and took them. Blankly, Griselda walked home, went into her kitchen, and showed her husband the delicious-looking ḥallot.

"It's strange, dear," she said, "very strange. When I went in, there was nothing in the oven, but suddenly…I tell you, I've been baking for forty years and I've never seen anything like it…"

And Rabbi Ḥanina's wife lifted her eyes up to heaven and whispered, "Thank You, dear God, for sending me such wonderful bread and saving me from such awful shame. I'm telling You, if it wasn't for miracles, I don't know how I'd cope in this house."

Based on Talmud Bavli, Ta'anit 24–25

Grandma's Shabbat Headscarf

Out of all the mitzvot that Rabbi Zakkai loved to keep, he loved to keep Shabbat most of all.

Out of all the mitzvot of Shabbat, he loved the Shabbat prayers most of all.

Out of all the Shabbat prayers, he loved the Kiddush most of all.

Rabbi Zakkai was as poor as they come. He wasn't married and he didn't have a family. Even his parents had died. The only person he had to love in the whole world was his grandmother. He loved her and she loved him. They lived together in a little cottage with walls so thin and crumbly that they might have been made of gingerbread. It was just as well that they weren't, because Rabbi Zakkai and his grandmother were often so hungry that if the walls had been made of gingerbread, they would have been eaten long ago. All week long, Rabbi Zakkai struggled to learn Torah and earn his living. He scrimped and saved and barely ate a thing. Why? Because he saved every penny he could spare to buy special foods in honor of Shabbat. Wine and ḥalla, fish and meat.

Sometimes, when he hadn't managed to scrape and scrimp and save enough, he didn't buy meat. Sometimes, he didn't have enough money for fish, either. He was *that* poor. But he never, ever, *ever* gave up on wine for Kiddush. When he made the blessing in a warm, loving voice, with Grandma wearing her special Shabbat headscarf and looking and listening with love, they forgot all their troubles. How could he bless the Shabbat without wine for Kiddush? He would often say, "Like salad needs a dressing, I need wine for the Kiddush blessing."

And even at the most desperate and destitute, impoverished and impecunious, needy and necessitous times (such rich words to describe such a poor man!), Rabbi Zakkai always made Kiddush. Always. There were days that Grandma would have to sell a beloved old necklace, or a pretty picture from the thin wall of their cottage. Sometimes Rabbi Zakkai would sell one of his few books. Anything but go without Kiddush!

And one dark, gloomy Friday, when the sun was sinking lower and lower behind the dark, gray clouds that loomed in the dark, gray sky, Rabbi Zakkai found that he had no money at all. Not two pennies to rub together. It had been a dark, wet week, and there were few buyers in the marketplace to buy Rabbi Zakkai's goods. And now Shabbat was drawing nearer. How would he buy wine for Kiddush? With a heavy heart, he went home to his grandma. She saw his long face and understood immediately. And with a heavy heart, she began to sift through her possessions.

Out of all her possessions, Grandma treasured her clothes most of all.

Out of all of her clothes, she loved her headscarves most of all.

Out of all of her headscarves, she had a favorite: a special, fine square of beautiful cloth that she loved to wear in honor of the Shabbat. Because she loved it so much, she had saved it, even

when they had nothing but bread to eat. But now, all her jewelry had been sold. All her paintings had been sold. All her fine clothes and scarves had been sold. All, but one! Her very favorite (though how can something not be your favorite, when it's the only one you have?), dearest, most special, Shabbat headscarf. She looked at it one last time, then slipped out to the marketplace when Rabbi Zakkai wasn't looking. Within minutes, she had sold it for enough money to buy meat and fish and crusty golden ḥallot for the Shabbat meals. And, of course, wine for Kiddush.

That Shabbat, as every Shabbat, Rabbi Zakkai made Kiddush. He watched Grandma looking at him and listening with love, as she did every week. But on her head she wore a very plain piece of cloth that looked suspiciously like one of her old dish towels. Where was her special and beautiful headscarf for Shabbat? He then understood that his grandmother had sold her last remaining treasured possession to buy wine for Kiddush. His voice filled with sorrow and regret for his grandmother's sacrifice as he finished the blessing. But her face shone with happiness and love. He wept for their poverty. But she smiled because in spite of their poverty, she had managed to fulfill the mitzva of Kiddush.

God in heaven looked down at their tears and their smiles, at their love for each other and their love for Shabbat. Before the next week had passed, before they could begin to worry about where to find wine for next week's Kiddush, He sent them great riches and blessed them with long lives. Many years later, when Grandma died, she left her grandson three hundred barrels of rich wine that would be enough for Rabbi Zakkai – and the whole village! – to make Kiddush for the rest of his life. And Rabbi Zakkai, who had since married a very nice woman and raised very nice children, was finally successful in business. Every Friday, Rabbi Zakkai and his children went out to distribute wine to all the poor people in the area, so that every family would be able to make Kiddush. No poor person in the village ever had to sell his possessions to buy a little wine for Kiddush.

"Because everything will be fine, when you make Kiddush on wine," rhymed Rabbi Zakkai happily every week, bouncing his grandchildren on his knee. His wife and children and grandchildren sat around the Shabbat table, wearing beautiful Shabbat clothes that Grandma would have loved.

Rabbi Zakkai lived a long, healthy and wealthy life. And when he died, he left his children over three thousand barrels of good rich wine. And ever since, his children and grandchildren and great-grandchildren enjoy a good glass of wine for Kiddush in honor of the Shabbat, while his daughters and granddaughters and great-granddaughters proudly wear the most fabulous Shabbat headscarves you've ever seen.

Based on Talmud Bavli, Megilla 27

Sweet and Sour –
A Prayer's Power

Rabbi Ḥanina Ben Dosa's daughter was very, very sad. Shabbat had just begun, but her face was not lit up with the glow of Shabbat joy and candles. Instead, her face was sad and gloomy.

Rabbi Ḥanina loved his daughter very much, but he was barely at home during the week. He was busy learning Torah and praying for the Jewish people. Some said that his prayers were so powerful that they flew up to God in heaven and God would lift up the little golden letters and answer them. Many people prayed and asked God for help – some prayed for health, some prayed for wealth. Some prayed for God to help them have children, some prayed for God to help them raise their children. Some prayed for things that weren't really that important. But Ḥanina never prayed for himself, only for the good of others.

Another week had gone by, and Shabbat had arrived. It is said that on Shabbat, every person gets a special extra soul inside of them that doubles their Shabbat joy. In that case, Rabbi Ḥanina's

family was triply happy on Shabbat, because they all got an extra soul, *and* Rabbi Ḥanina was finally home! At last, it was the special time for the whole family to gather around the Shabbat table, with their faces glowing and the candles glowing, and no one could be sure if the candles or the faces were brighter. The family spent all Friday preparing for Shabbat. The older children would wash the dishes, and the younger children would put away their toys and help their mother cook. To be precise, their mother would cook and the children would help taste. And the daughter we told you about before, who was smack in the middle, between the older kids washing and the little kids tasting, had a special job that was only hers: she was in charge of preparing the candles for lighting. She would prepare the oil for the shiny silver candleholders, so that the lights would shine all through the Shabbat meal.

Oh, how she loved Shabbat. She was so proud of the soft glow that filled the house all evening. Her mother would light the wicks floating in the oil and say, "How beautifully you glow, my daughter!" Her father would come home after the Shabbat evening prayers and say to her, "You are the light that fills our home!"

But now, as the sun set, her eyes filled with tears instead of light. "What happened, my daughter? Why are you so sad?" asked Rabbi Ḥanina. She answered in a low, embarrassed voice, "I've made an awful mistake! Instead of buying oil for the Shabbat candles, I bought vinegar! I only realized my mistake once I'd poured it into the candleholders – the bottles look so similar that I mixed them up! The candles shine so beautifully with oil, but they won't shine at all with vinegar! Now, because of me, we'll have to sit here all evening in the dark!" And she burst into tears. (You must remember that this happened centuries before electricity was invented, and the Shabbat candles were the only light shining in their home on Friday night.)

Rabbi Ḥanina smiled and said, "My dear girl, don't get yourself into such a state! So you poured in vinegar instead of oil. No big deal. If God can make oil burn, He can surely make vinegar burn. He who told the oil to burn, will just tell the vinegar to burn instead! Really, there's no reason to be sad!"

The words had barely left his mouth when the wicks floating in their little dishes of vinegar suddenly sparked a glowing orange flame. Because when Rabbi Ḥanina asked something of God – God wouldn't refuse him. And if Rabbi Ḥanina wanted his daughter to

cheer up – God was happy to cheer her up. Who wouldn't go out of his way to make a little girl happy, particularly if the little girl was Rabbi Ḥanina ben Dosa's daughter?

"Just this once, we'll use vinegar for something besides salad dressing!" said Rabbi Ḥanina.

People whispered that on that special Shabbat, the candles glowed brightly from Friday night until three stars twinkled in the sky on Saturday evening. Much, much longer than candles that burn with oil. And Rabbi Ḥanina's daughter glowed just as brightly.

The smile was back on the little girl's face, and she smiled even more when her father asked her: "Would you please make me a cup of coffee? Two sugars please – only, if you don't mind, try not to mix up the sugar and the salt. I'm not sure I could manage another miracle today…"

Based on Talmud Bavli, Ta'anit 25

About the Author

Uri Orbach is an Israeli journalist, media personality and member of Knesset. He was a founder of the leading Israeli children's magazine, *Otiyot*, the religious television station, *Tekhelet*, and the radio station, *Kol Ḥai*. He is widely known as a regular columnist for Israel's largest newspaper, *Yedioth Ahronoth*.

Maggid Books offer the best of contemporary Jewish thought from renowned rabbis, scholars, philosophers and halakhic experts around the world. Published in English and Hebrew, Maggid books provide new approaches to Jewish texts and themes. Maggid is an imprint of Koren Publishers Jerusalem: **www.korenpub.com**